STECK-VAUGHN

TEST BEST

Stanford
Tenth Edition

ISBN 0-7398-8806-4

© 2004 Harcourt Achieve Inc.

Printed in the United States of America.

2 3 4 5 6 7 8 9 10 030 10 09 08 07 06 05 04

Harcourt Achieve

Rigby • Steck-Vaughn

www.HarcourtAchieve.com
1.800.531.5015

Table of Contents

INFORMATIONAL READING COMPREHENSION

Skill Focus Lessons

FUNCTIONAL READING COMPREHENSION

Skill Focus Lessons

PRACTICE POSTTEST FOR STANFORD 10
Test Battery, Primary 3 Level

Word Study Skills

DIRECTIONS ▶

In each question, there are three words. Decide which word is a compound word. Then mark the space for the answer you have chosen.

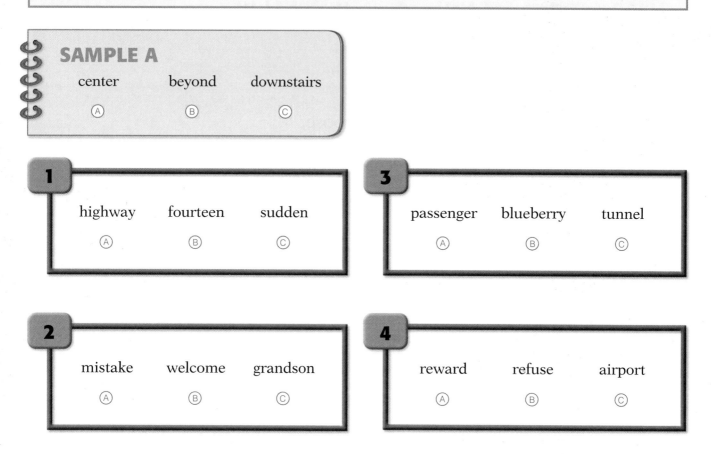

SAMPLE A

center	beyond	downstairs
Ⓐ	Ⓑ	Ⓒ

1

highway	fourteen	sudden
Ⓐ	Ⓑ	Ⓒ

3

passenger	blueberry	tunnel
Ⓐ	Ⓑ	Ⓒ

2

mistake	welcome	grandson
Ⓐ	Ⓑ	Ⓒ

4

reward	refuse	airport
Ⓐ	Ⓑ	Ⓒ

DIRECTIONS ▶

Read each question and choose the best answer. Then mark the space for the answer you have chosen.

SAMPLE B

The <u>un</u> in <u>unusual</u> means the same as the <u>im</u> in —

imagine   impolite   important

ⓐ   ⓑ   ©

5

tran<u>sport</u>   im<u>port</u>   ex<u>port</u>

<u>trans</u> means <u>across</u>
<u>im</u> means <u>into</u>
<u>ex</u> means <u>out of</u>

The word part <u>port</u> must have something to do with —

carry   lean   talk

ⓐ   ⓑ   ©

6

<u>tele</u>phone   <u>tele</u>gram   <u>tele</u>vision

The word part <u>tele</u> must have something to do with —

pull   see   far

ⓐ   ⓑ   ©

7

The <u>or</u> in <u>conductor</u> means the same as the <u>er</u> in —

enter   spider   player

ⓐ   ⓑ   ©

8

The <u>hood</u> in <u>childhood</u> means the same as the <u>ment</u> in —

enjoyment   moment   cement

ⓐ   ⓑ   ©

9

The <u>dis</u> in <u>disappear</u> means the same as the <u>in</u> in —

insect   invite   incomplete

Ⓐ   Ⓑ   Ⓒ

11

In which word does <u>mis</u> mean <u>wrong</u>?

missile   mission   misuse

Ⓐ   Ⓑ   Ⓒ

10

In which word does <u>re</u> mean <u>again</u>?

receive   rewrite   rescue

Ⓐ   Ⓑ   Ⓒ

12

In which word does <u>less</u> mean <u>without</u>?

lesson   blessing   careless

Ⓐ   Ⓑ   Ⓒ

DIRECTIONS ▶

Look at the word with the underlined letter or letters. The underlined letter or letters stand for a sound. Decide which of the other three words has the same sound in it. Then mark the space for the answer you have chosen.

SAMPLE C

am<u>u</u>se

tune	puff	upon
Ⓐ	Ⓑ	Ⓒ

15

<u>o</u>cean

whole	possible	closet
Ⓐ	Ⓑ	Ⓒ

13

<u>a</u>mong

candy	gaze	canary
Ⓐ	Ⓑ	Ⓒ

16

ch<u>a</u>tter

save	awful	narrow
Ⓐ	Ⓑ	Ⓒ

14

<u>i</u>sland

sixty	nibble	dime
Ⓐ	Ⓑ	Ⓒ

17

b<u>a</u>ggage

against	patch	nation
Ⓐ	Ⓑ	Ⓒ

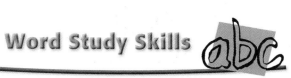

18

m<u>ea</u>nt

heart   eagle   peddler

Ⓐ   Ⓑ   Ⓒ

22

ch<u>ee</u>se

feast   sleigh   pencil

Ⓐ   Ⓑ   Ⓒ

19

pa<u>g</u>e

guard   gentle   gift

Ⓐ   Ⓑ   Ⓒ

23

<u>g</u>uide

giant   giraffe   gather

Ⓐ   Ⓑ   Ⓒ

20

<u>f</u>aithful

package   matter   waste

Ⓐ   Ⓑ   Ⓒ

24

<u>c</u>ontest

toss   often   pond

Ⓐ   Ⓑ   Ⓒ

21

t<u>ou</u>ch

bunch   food   loud

Ⓐ   Ⓑ   Ⓒ

25

<u>c</u>ertainly

carve   circle   coach

Ⓐ   Ⓑ   Ⓒ

26

u̲nit

cure   lump   judge

Ⓐ   Ⓑ   Ⓒ

29

ri̲bbon

slide   written   iron

Ⓐ   Ⓑ   Ⓒ

27

arri̲ve

piano   till   lively

Ⓐ   Ⓑ   Ⓒ

30

blo̲ssom

worm   plow   hollow

Ⓐ   Ⓑ   Ⓒ

28

co̲conut

none   trot   broke

Ⓐ   Ⓑ   Ⓒ

Reading Vocabulary

Choose the word or group of words that means the same, or about the same, as the underlined word. Then mark the space for the answer you have chosen.

SAMPLE A

To <u>yell</u> means to —

(A) say   (C) whisper

(B) shout   (D) sniff

1

A <u>fact</u> is a —

(A) truth   (C) piece

(B) word   (D) pen

2

<u>Cattle</u> are —

(A) groups   (C) cows

(B) cats   (D) bees

3

An <u>insect</u> is a —

(A) bug   (C) fish

(B) bird   (D) lizard

4

<u>Smart</u> means —

(A) good   (C) proud

(B) happy   (D) wise

5

A <u>boot</u> is most like a —

(A) sock   (C) coat

(B) shoe   (D) belt

6

A <u>cliff</u> is a —

ⓐ river   ⓒ ledge

ⓑ sea   ⓓ valley

10

To <u>soothe</u> means to —

ⓐ calm   ⓒ stir

ⓑ please   ⓓ hurt

7

<u>Certainly</u> means —

ⓐ hardly   ⓒ surely

ⓑ friendly   ⓓ usually

11

To <u>soar</u> is to —

ⓐ reach   ⓒ leave

ⓑ rain   ⓓ fly

8

To <u>dine</u> is to —

ⓐ eat   ⓒ stride

ⓑ sing   ⓓ giggle

12

To <u>bother</u> is to —

ⓐ trouble   ⓒ move

ⓑ anger   ⓓ hate

9

<u>Breezy</u> means —

ⓐ dirty   ⓒ angry

ⓑ happy   ⓓ windy

DIRECTIONS ▶

Read the sentence in the box. Then choose the answer in which the underlined word is used in the same way. Mark the space for the answer you have chosen.

SAMPLE B

Rosa will play outside after she does her homework.

In which sentence does the word play mean the same as in the sentence above?

Ⓐ They watched their mom play tennis.

Ⓑ Tanya went to see her sister's play.

Ⓒ The teacher said that we must play by the rules.

Ⓓ Jerome's father told him not to play with his food.

14

Brad liked the new head of his scout group.

In which sentence does the word head mean the same as in the sentence above?

Ⓐ He patted the dog on the head.

Ⓑ Our teacher did a head count to make sure everyone was in the room.

Ⓒ Jim walked to the head of the line.

Ⓓ Our teacher was the head of the music club.

13

Laura did not act happy.

In which sentence does the word act mean the same as in the sentence above?

Ⓐ Hugo would always act calm.

Ⓑ Her anger was just an act.

Ⓒ John will act in the play.

Ⓓ Helping Olivia was an act of kindness.

15

My mother says reading is food for the mind.

In which sentence does the word mind mean the same as in the sentence above?

Ⓐ Do you mind if I have an apple?

Ⓑ It was my job to mind my baby sister.

Ⓒ She speaks her mind at every meeting.

Ⓓ The scientist had a great mind.

16

I take <u>care</u> of my mother when she is sick.

In which sentence does the word <u>care</u> mean the same as in the sentence above?

(A) My goldfish does not have a <u>care</u> in the world.

(B) He does not <u>care</u> if she sits in his seat.

(C) Gary's daily job is to <u>care</u> for the dog.

(D) Take <u>care</u> to lock the door when you leave.

17

Brandon tried to <u>bat</u> at the flies circling around his head.

In which sentence does the word <u>bat</u> mean the same as in the sentence above?

(A) The bird learned to <u>bat</u> its wings.

(B) The kitten did not <u>bat</u> the little butterfly.

(C) The <u>bat</u> flew into the cave.

(D) I got a new baseball <u>bat</u>.

18

Hold hands and form a <u>ring</u>.

In which sentence does the word <u>ring</u> mean the same as in the sentence above?

(A) Ryan waited for the bell to <u>ring</u>.

(B) Draw a <u>ring</u> around the right answer.

(C) Chang wears a gold <u>ring</u> on his finger.

(D) The wrestlers climbed into the <u>ring</u>.

19

Ricky was a football <u>star</u>.

In which sentence does the word <u>star</u> mean the same as in the sentence above?

(A) Amy wanted to <u>star</u> in the show.

(B) The teacher put a <u>star</u> on my chart.

(C) The Sun is really a <u>star</u>.

(D) That movie made her a <u>star</u>.

20

After the test, my grade <u>rose</u> to an A.

In which sentence does the word <u>rose</u> mean the same as in the sentence above?

Ⓐ The class <u>rose</u> to clap at the end of the play.

Ⓑ Lei only had one <u>rose</u> in her garden.

Ⓒ The temperature <u>rose</u> to 90 degrees.

Ⓓ On school days, I <u>rose</u> at 6:00 A.M.

21

<u>Face</u> the front of the class.

In which sentence does the word <u>face</u> mean the same as in the sentence above?

Ⓐ Sara made a funny <u>face</u> when she saw her dinner.

Ⓑ The cat licked her paws to wash her <u>face</u>.

Ⓒ For the next dance step, <u>face</u> your partner.

Ⓓ You must <u>face</u> your fears.

DIRECTIONS ▶

As you read each sentence, use the other words in the sentence to help you figure out what the underlined word means. Then mark the space for the answer you have chosen.

SAMPLE C

Donato's <u>dream</u> is to be a basketball player. <u>Dream</u> means —

Ⓐ   thought   Ⓒ   fear

Ⓑ   hope   Ⓓ   amusement

22

The ship was both <u>broad</u> and long. <u>Broad</u> means —

Ⓐ plain

Ⓑ clean

Ⓒ wide

Ⓓ small

23

We saw the deer quickly <u>dart</u> across the lawn. <u>Dart</u> means —

Ⓐ wander

Ⓑ dash

Ⓒ stroll

Ⓓ dance

24

When the dog barked, the rabbit <u>vanished</u> from sight. <u>Vanished</u> means —

Ⓐ disappeared

Ⓑ hopped

Ⓒ marched

Ⓓ walked

25

I am happy that you had a <u>fabulous</u> time at the party! <u>Fabulous</u> means —

Ⓐ boring

Ⓑ scary

Ⓒ terrible

Ⓓ wonderful

26

We can <u>sample</u> a piece of cake to see what it tastes like. <u>Sample</u> means —

Ⓐ try

Ⓑ smash

Ⓒ cool

Ⓓ shake

29

The teacher was <u>furious</u> when the computer crashed. <u>Furious</u> means —

Ⓐ overjoyed

Ⓑ mad

Ⓒ nervous

Ⓓ happy

27

Now that it is <u>definite</u> that we have a holiday, let's make plans. <u>Definite</u> means —

Ⓐ wrong

Ⓑ safe

Ⓒ sure

Ⓓ often

30

The <u>author</u> of the book told us how she came up with her ideas. <u>Author</u> means —

Ⓐ seller

Ⓑ reader

Ⓒ buyer

Ⓓ writer

28

The <u>cheerful</u> child smiled most of the time. <u>Cheerful</u> means —

Ⓐ sick

Ⓑ sleepy

Ⓒ small

Ⓓ happy

Reading Comprehension

Read each passage. Then read each question about the passage. Decide which is the best answer to the question. Mark the space for the answer you have chosen.

SAMPLES

The Good Bad Habit

One day Ricky's mother saw him throwing food scraps into the garden. She said, "Ricky, you're a litterbug! Don't you know that ants will come?" Ricky didn't like ants. "And don't you know that worms will come?" his mother said. Ricky kind of liked worms. "Raccoons might come, too," his mother said. "Raccoons might come to eat your food scraps."

Ricky wanted to see raccoons. He watched for them. None came. He looked at the garden. Then he dug into the dirt. He watched the long, healthy earthworms wriggle through the dirt.

Ricky ate a snack in the garden every day. He threw his food scraps into the dirt. He watched the worms wriggle around. The dirt got thicker and richer. Ricky's mother was pleased. "In this case, Ricky, being a litterbug was a good thing. The worms broke down your food scraps and fed the soil. Now we have good, rich compost. It will help our garden grow." Ricky was pleased, too. "I always wanted compost to use in our garden," said Ricky's mother. "I always kind of liked worms!" said Ricky.

A

How were worms good for Ricky's garden?

- Ⓐ They fed the soil.
- Ⓑ They fed raccoons.
- Ⓒ They grew big and healthy.
- Ⓓ They wriggled through the dirt.

B

This passage teaches us mainly —

- Ⓐ how to make a garden
- Ⓑ how to make compost
- Ⓒ that Ricky likes worms
- Ⓓ that Ricky is a litterbug

Why Bear Has a Stubby Tail

One cold winter afternoon, Fox searched the forest for food. Fox was hungry and he felt discouraged.

"Fiddlesticks!" Fox shouted, as he watched a speedy rabbit escape. "I'll go to the river and see what animals I can find there."

Fox saw Bear sitting on the riverbank with his back to Fox. When he got closer, Fox saw that Bear was fishing.

"Are you catching anything?" Fox asked when he noticed Bear stirring the water with his huge paws.

"I just swallowed a tasty trout," Bear bragged, "but it was too small and I'm still hungry. I'm going to catch another one."

Fox decided to trick Bear. Bear was bigger than Fox, but Fox was smarter. Fox knew that Bear had not found a use for his tail.

"Isn't it tiring to bend over and fish with your paws?" Fox asked, swishing his bushy tail. "Why don't you use your long, skinny tail?" "I'll splash in the river and scare the fish your way," Fox explained. "You wiggle your tail and yank the fish out when they bite it."

Bear agreed to Fox's plan. One after the other, dozens of fish bit Bear's tail. Each time, he flung them onto the riverbank behind him.

When the sun went down, the water began to freeze around Bear's tail. He did not see Fox sneak behind him and steal the fish.

Finally, Bear shouted, "Fox, thanks for your help. I'm going to take my fish and leave." Only then did he discover that Fox had stolen all of his food. Bear was very upset.

He jumped up to go home. His long tail, which was stuck in the ice, popped off. That's why Bear has a stubby tail.

1

You would *most likely* read this story to be —

Ⓐ persuaded

Ⓑ entertained

Ⓒ educated

Ⓓ informed

2

Which detail from the story shows why Bear agreed to Fox's plan?

Ⓐ Bear was bigger than Fox, but Fox was smarter.

Ⓑ Fox knew that Bear would not share his fish.

Ⓒ Bear's long tail popped off when he jumped up.

Ⓓ Bear had not yet found a use for his long tail.

3

One way Bear and Fox are alike is that they both —

Ⓐ like to catch fish

Ⓑ like to steal food

Ⓒ have long, skinny tails

Ⓓ are very hungry

4

Fox thought he could trick Bear because —

Ⓐ he was smarter than Bear

Ⓑ he was smaller than Bear

Ⓒ Bear was hungry

Ⓓ Bear was selfish

5

This story was *most likely* written for —

Ⓐ art students

Ⓑ science teachers

Ⓒ people who like to fish

Ⓓ people who like animals

6

Because this story tells the events in the order they happened, we know we'll understand what the title means —

Ⓐ at the beginning of the story

Ⓑ in the middle of the story

Ⓒ at the end of the story

Ⓓ when we read the title

Pictures in the Sky

Do you like to look at stars on dark nights? If you live in a city, you cannot always see stars, but if you live out in the country you might see a lot of them. The sky is very dark in the country, and the stars look like little dots of light. If you draw lines between the dots, you can make pictures. You can make dot-to-dot pictures in the sky!

People who watched the sky long ago gave names to the pictures they made. People all over the world made dot-to-dot pictures in the sky. We call these pictures *constellations* (kän-stah-LAY-shahnz). Many of the pictures looked like animals, such as dogs and bears. People drew pictures of these animals to make maps of the sky. These maps helped people remember where the stars were when they looked at the sky on dark nights.

People who lived long ago saw a dark sky every night. The only light they had came from the moon and the stars. On nights this dark, the sky looked like a blackboard filled with dots. There were so many dots that it was impossible to tell them apart! That is why people drew lines between them and made pictures. Drawing lines between the dots helped people make a picture book of the night sky.

Today, people use the picture book in the sky as a sky map. People who study the stars use sky maps to find certain stars and learn what they are made of and how far away the stars are from Earth. People who study the stars are called astronomers (uh-STRON-uh-muhrz). Astronomers find star maps very useful. You might want to use a star map, too. If you have a chance to look at a dark night sky, you can find the stars when you read the picture book that people made long ago.

7

People drew pictures with the stars to —

(A) watch stars at work

(B) see dots of light

(C) make maps of the sky

(D) find skies that were dark

10

After reading the passage, what can you say is true of people long ago?

(A) They liked to draw.

(B) They used the stars to guide them.

(C) They did not like cities.

(D) They read lots of books.

8

If you want to see pictures in the stars, it is important to know that you can —

(A) live in the country

(B) be an astronomer

(C) use a sky map

(D) learn how to draw

11

What does the author think the reader might like to do?

(A) Watch the stars

(B) Draw some animals

(C) Read good books

(D) Stay up late

9

This passage is *mainly* about —

(A) going outside

(B) seeing stars

(C) reading books

(D) seeing animals

12

Which paragraph explains how people study stars?

(A) The first paragraph

(B) The second paragraph

(C) The third paragraph

(D) The fourth paragraph

The Life Cycle of the Butterfly

Egg
A mother butterfly lays many eggs on leaves. Each egg is tiny and looks like this one. The leaves that are around it will become its food when it hatches.

Butterfly
The butterfly comes out from the chrysalis. It will travel to other places and look for another butterfly for its mate. After mating, the mother butterfly lays her eggs on leaves. Then, the life cycle of the butterfly will begin again.

Caterpillar
The caterpillar is also called a larva (LAR-vuh). It hatches from the egg and begins eating leaves that are all around it. It might have patches of color. Some caterpillars have little hairs. As the caterpillar grows, it sheds its skin four or more times.

Chrysalis
After the caterpillar sheds its skin for the last time, it stays inside a hard shell called a chrysalis (KRIH-suh-luhs). The chrysalis is also called the pupa (PYOO-puh). Inside the chrysalis, the caterpillar is resting and changing its body into a butterfly's body.

13

The caterpillar changes while it is a —

Ⓐ tiny egg

Ⓑ caterpillar

Ⓒ chrysalis

Ⓓ butterfly

14

Why does a mother butterfly lay her eggs on leaves?

Ⓐ To place them near food

Ⓑ To help her find them later

Ⓒ To keep them warm and dry

Ⓓ To hide them from other creatures

15

This poster describes the life cycle of the butterfly from —

Ⓐ caterpillar to butterfly

Ⓑ chrysalis to butterfly

Ⓒ egg to butterfly

Ⓓ egg to caterpillar

16

The butterfly eats the most when it is a —

Ⓐ tiny egg

Ⓑ caterpillar

Ⓒ chrysalis

Ⓓ butterfly

17

This poster can help you to —

Ⓐ learn what a butterfly eats

Ⓑ learn what plants attract a butterfly

Ⓒ see how a butterfly flies

Ⓓ learn how a butterfly grows

18

How many changes does a butterfly go through in its life cycle?

Ⓐ Four

Ⓑ Three

Ⓒ Two

Ⓓ One

The Backyard Adventure

Maria glared at her sleeping friend. "How can Annie sleep through this?" she grumbled again. She pretended to accidentally roll over and bump Annie. Maria sighed and cleared her throat loudly. Didn't Annie know that you weren't supposed to sleep at a sleepover? Apparently she didn't. Annie just snored and coughed. "Her allergy medicine has made her very tired," Maria thought. "Why did I agree to camp out in Annie's yard tonight?" Annie's mother had wanted to postpone the sleepover for an evening when her daughter was feeling better.

Maria thought about the evening. It had started out fine. First, they ate grilled chicken with Annie's family. Then they told scary stories. Finally, they took flashlights and books to their tent, but the fun was over. Annie fell asleep without even opening her book.

Now it was late and Annie's sisters had gone to bed. Suddenly, Maria heard a noise. It sounded different from the wind or Annie's snores. It was a swishing, crunching sound. It was an animal! Maria was sure of it. Could it be her dog? Or could it be a raccoon in Annie's yard?

"Annie! Annie! Wake up!" she whispered. "There's something coming toward our tent. It sounds like a raccoon."

"Huh?" said Annie. "What?"

"Annie!" Maria whispered urgently. "Wake up. Where is your flashlight? I think there's a raccoon outside the tent!" The crunching sound came closer. It swished right up to the tent. Maria thought it might scurry inside, looking for food. Then she heard a voice.

"Annie," the voice said. "I brought you a handkerchief."

Maria sighed with relief as she saw Annie's mom look inside the tent. The evening had been exciting after all!

19

The writer *most likely* wants you to —

Ⓐ feel frustrated about camping

Ⓑ understand why Annie is sleepy

Ⓒ laugh about Maria's vivid imagination

Ⓓ feel scared about a raccoon

20

Just before she hears the voice at the end of the story, Maria is feeling —

Ⓐ excited

Ⓑ unhappy

Ⓒ bored

Ⓓ worried

21

This story is *mainly* about how —

Ⓐ Annie fell asleep early

Ⓑ Maria's imagination tricked her

Ⓒ Maria and Annie told ghost stories

Ⓓ Annie's mother tried to postpone the sleepover

22

Why does Maria first try to wake Annie?

Ⓐ She is tired.

Ⓑ She is bored.

Ⓒ She is still hungry.

Ⓓ She wants to go inside.

23

This passage is a —

Ⓐ folktale

Ⓑ fantasy

Ⓒ mystery

Ⓓ short story

24

If you do not know the meaning of *postpone* in the first paragraph, you should —

Ⓐ find out if the word is a verb

Ⓑ break the word into syllables

Ⓒ read on, looking for clues

Ⓓ look at the word before it

The Monterey Bay Aquarium

The oceans are full of amazing animals. Sadly, a lot of these animals are in danger. To save these animals, we must learn more about them. The Monterey Bay Aquarium is a good place to learn about sea animals. You can also find out what you can do to protect them. Many of the sea animals in the Aquarium live in the kelp forest of Monterey Bay.

What is a kelp forest? Kelp is a kind of algae called seaweed. In many parts of the ocean, algae carpet the sea floor. A kelp forest is an area of the ocean that is covered with giant kelps. The kelp forest provides food and protection for many kinds of sea animals.

Who lives in a kelp forest? The kelp forest is home to many different kinds of fish and other ocean animals. Sea otters and sea turtles live in the kelp forest. Sharks and tuna also live in the kelp forest. Some of these animals swim in the water close to the coast. Others swim in the water farther away from shore.

Why are these animals in danger? Some kinds of tuna and shark are in danger because people do too much fishing for these animals. Sea otters are in danger because of disease and oil spills. Sea turtles are in danger because they often get caught in fishing nets and lines that are used to trap other animals.

What can we do to help them? Scientists work every day to protect the life in the oceans. You can help, too. If you want to help sea animals, you can learn about how they live and how they find food. You can learn how to rescue sea animals that get trapped. You can help them by visiting the Monterey Bay Aquarium in person. Tell people about the things you saw on your visit to the Aquarium. You will teach people about important ways they can protect sea animals.

25

What is the *best* way to learn quickly what the passage is about?

Ⓐ Read the passage quickly.

Ⓑ Read the last paragraph first.

Ⓒ Read the parts in heavy, dark print.

Ⓓ Read the whole passage carefully.

28

Why does the author say that algae *carpet* the sea floor?

Ⓐ They color the sea floor.

Ⓑ They soften the sea floor.

Ⓒ They warm the sea floor.

Ⓓ They cover the sea floor.

26

According to the passage, what is causing danger to sea turtles?

Ⓐ Oil spills

Ⓑ Disease

Ⓒ Too much fishing

Ⓓ Fishing nets and lines

29

The passage was *most likely* written by someone who —

Ⓐ likes to tell stories

Ⓑ works at the Aquarium

Ⓒ swims in the ocean

Ⓓ grows kelp for the forest

27

Based on what you learned in the passage, what is true about the Monterey Bay Aquarium?

Ⓐ It has classes for children.

Ⓑ It has seahorses and crabs.

Ⓒ It helps protect sea animals.

Ⓓ It helps sea turtles find food.

30

The passage is *mainly* about —

Ⓐ saving sea animals

Ⓑ fishing in the bay

Ⓒ going to the Aquarium

Ⓓ living in the ocean

Funny Bones Café

"We'll Make You Smile"

Kid's Menu - For children 10 and under only, please.
All meals come with our special air fries.

Corny Corn Dog $2.99
It's no joke!

Hilarious Hot Dog $2.99
A ha-ha-happy time!

Funny Burger $2.99
Laughing all the way home!

Barrel-O-Burgers $2.99
Six mini-burgers in our own "Barrel-O-Laughs"!

Funny-Face Pancake $2.99
This will make you break out in smiles!

Chuckling Cheese Sandwich $2.99
Cheer up with grilled Texas toast and real cheese!

Silly Spaghetti $2.99
Stir up some fun with our goofy garlic bread! *Spaghetti served plain or with red sauce!*

Side-Splitting Side Orders

Goofy Garlic Bread $1.50
Two thick slices of our special bread!

Air-Head Air Fries $1.50
Can you handle the fun?

Drinks

Monkey Shine Smoothies $1.00
Choo Choo Cherry • Laughing Lime • Chipper Chocolate • Very Funny Vanilla

Milk $1.00

Chocolate milk $1.00

Orange juice $1.00

Dreamy Desserts

Simon Says Sundae $1.50

Belly–Laugh Brownie $1.50

31

The Funny Bones Café Kid's Menu helps you —

Ⓐ talk to your parents at lunch

Ⓑ learn about vegetables

Ⓒ order a meal

Ⓓ color your menu

32

The people who can order from this menu must be —

Ⓐ 65 or under

Ⓑ 40 or under

Ⓒ 18 or under

Ⓓ 10 or under

33

Based on the menu, the cost of apple juice would *probably* be —

Ⓐ $5.00

Ⓑ $3.00

Ⓒ $2.00

Ⓓ $1.00

34

A menu should list —

Ⓐ jokes and food

Ⓑ food and cost

Ⓒ jokes and things to color

Ⓓ food and things to color

35

Based on the menu, the <u>barrel</u> in a "Barrel-O-Burgers" is *most* like a —

Ⓐ sack

Ⓑ basket

Ⓒ bucket

Ⓓ plate

36

On the menu, the pancake is called "Funny-Face" probably because it —

Ⓐ looks like a face

Ⓑ gets on your face

Ⓒ comes with a joke

Ⓓ tastes funny

Flight Lessons

The eaglets flap their little wings.

They're learning how to fly.

From nest to branch and back again,

they try and try and try.

5   Their parents teach them patiently.

The eaglets rarely rest.

They'll soon learn to soar and hunt,

and then they'll leave the nest.

37

In what order do eaglets grow up?

Ⓐ They hunt, leave the nest, learn to fly, and then fly.

Ⓑ They leave the nest, hunt, fly, and learn to fly.

Ⓒ They fly, leave the nest, learn to fly, and hunt.

Ⓓ They learn to fly, fly, hunt, and leave the nest.

38

You can tell that the eaglets —

Ⓐ are sad to leave their parents

Ⓑ have a lot of energy

Ⓒ are glad their parents teach them

Ⓓ like to sleep in the nest

39

After the eaglets can fly and hunt, they will —

Ⓐ be able to care for themselves

Ⓑ depend on their parents

Ⓒ continue learning to fly

Ⓓ continue living in the nest

40

Because "Flight Lessons" is made up of two groups of sentences, you can tell it is a —

Ⓐ short story

Ⓑ poem

Ⓒ folktale

Ⓓ mystery

41

"Flight Lessons" was *most likely* written for —

Ⓐ children

Ⓑ bird watchers

Ⓒ bird owners

Ⓓ poets

42

"Flight Lessons" is made up of —

Ⓐ lines

Ⓑ directions

Ⓒ paragraphs

Ⓓ chapters

The Baobab Tree

Imagine a tree that grows upside down! The baobab tree does not really grow upside down, but it looks like it does. Its branches are so twisted that they look like roots. Imagine a tree so big that you can live inside it. The trunk of the baobab tree is so thick that people have hollowed the trunks out to make homes.

The baobab tree is one of the largest trees in the world and probably the most unusual. The tree grows in Africa, and people in Africa have told legends for thousands of years to explain this tree. Legends help people explain things they cannot understand.

People in Africa tell different legends about the baobab tree. Some legends explain how the tree protects people from harm. Other legends of the baobab tree explain why it looks upside down. One legend says that an animal called Hyena planted it upside down to play a trick on nature. Another legend says that the tree got what it deserved for moaning and complaining when it wanted something different than what it had.

In this legend, the baobab was the first tree in the world. It was happy with itself until the palm tree came along. The baobab tree wanted to be tall like the palm tree. The baobab tree moaned and complained. Then the flame tree came along. The baobab tree wanted to have bright red flowers like the flame tree. It moaned and complained some more. Moaning and complaining did not help the baobab tree get what it wanted at all! It did not grow taller, and it did not get bright red flowers. It got turned upside down. Now, with its head in the ground and its roots in the air, the baobab tree cannot moan and complain any more!

43

What did the author *mainly* want to teach you by writing the passage?

Ⓐ That Africa has trees

Ⓑ That people tell legends

Ⓒ That legends explain things

Ⓓ That baobabs have thick trunks

44

According to legend, why did Hyena plant the tree upside down?

Ⓐ To help it grow taller

Ⓑ To play a trick on nature

Ⓒ To twist the tree's branches

Ⓓ To help it grow bright red leaves

45

What is *most* important to know in order to understand why people believed the baobab tree could protect them?

Ⓐ The roots stick up in the air.

Ⓑ The branches are twisted.

Ⓒ The trunk provides shelter.

Ⓓ The tree is unusual.

46

Based on the passage, how does the baobab tree *most likely* make the people of Africa feel?

Ⓐ Thankful

Ⓑ Curious

Ⓒ Alive

Ⓓ Lonely

47

In the legend of the baobab tree, what words make the tree seem like a person?

Ⓐ "Growing upside down"

Ⓑ "Living inside"

Ⓒ "Moaning and complaining"

Ⓓ "Playing a trick on nature"

48

What does the author explain about the baobab tree in the first paragraph?

Ⓐ Why it is unusual

Ⓑ Why it complained

Ⓒ Why it has a thick trunk

Ⓓ Why it was planted upside down

Pen Pals

Jack Douglas
400 Spruce Lane
Elk Grove Village, IL 40216

November 28, 2003

Colin Archer
63 North Charing Cross
London, UK EC1V0HL

Dear Colin,

Today my teacher, Mrs. Grant, announced that our class will be pen pals with your class. Her friend, Ms. Edmond, is your teacher. Ms. Edmond gave my teacher the names of the boys and girls in your class. Mrs. Grant put all the names in a box and let us each pick a name. I picked yours. Would you like to be a pen pal?

I am eight years old. In my family, I have my mom, my dad, my younger brother, and me. Who is in your family? Here is picture of myself. I live in Elk Grove Village. It is near Chicago. Chicago is a big city. How big is London?

Do you like soccer? Mrs. Grant said that soccer is called football in England. I am on a soccer team named the Eagles. My coach is Mr. Sanders. I practice after school on Tuesdays and Thursdays. On Saturdays, I have games. I usually play goalie, but sometimes I play forward. What is your favorite sport?

I have two pets. One is my dog, Sam. He is a beagle. I have had him as long as I can remember, so he is getting old for a dog. My other pet is my lizard, named Slinky. Do you have any pets?

I am writing this letter for my English class, but I hope you will write back to me. If you write to me, I will write you back.

Your Pen Pal,

Jack Douglas

49

How did Jack get Colin's name and the address of his school?

Ⓐ From Jack's pen pal, Colin

Ⓑ From Jack's teacher, Mrs. Grant

Ⓒ From Jack's coach, Mr. Sanders

Ⓓ From Jack's teacher, Ms. Edmond

50

According to the letter, how old could Sam, Jack's dog, be?

Ⓐ 1

Ⓑ 3

Ⓒ 5

Ⓓ 8

51

What is the main idea of the fourth paragraph?

Ⓐ Slinky's skin

Ⓑ Sam the dog

Ⓒ Jack's pets

Ⓓ Eagles

52

Based on the information in the third paragraph, what will Jack do next Tuesday?

Ⓐ Take Sam for a walk after school

Ⓑ Play in a soccer game

Ⓒ Practice with his soccer team

Ⓓ Play a football game

53

Jack wrote the letter to Colin because —

Ⓐ it was an assignment for his English class

Ⓑ he wanted to thank Ms. Edmond for his pen pal

Ⓒ he wanted to ask for an English football

Ⓓ it was Colin's birthday

54

If Jack wants to put a question in every paragraph, what question should he add to paragraph five?

Ⓐ Have you ever been to Chicago?

Ⓑ What is your favorite football team?

Ⓒ Do you like cats?

Ⓓ Will you write back soon?

Word Study Skills

Structural Analysis: Recognizing Compound Words

A compound word is a word that is made when two smaller words are put together to make a new word. For example, the word <u>rain</u> can be combined with the word <u>fall</u> to make the compound word <u>rainfall</u>.

To figure out the meaning of a compound word, think about the meaning of the two smaller words that make up the compound word. What is the meaning of <u>rainfall</u>? The word <u>rain</u> refers to water that is formed in the sky. The word <u>fall</u> means "coming down." Therefore, the compound word <u>rainfall</u> means "water coming down from the sky."

Sometimes a word looks like a compound word because it has two smaller parts. Think about the word <u>beyond</u>, for example. The two smaller parts of the word are <u>be</u> and <u>yond</u>. <u>Be</u> is a word, but <u>yond</u> is not a word. <u>Beyond</u> is not a compound word.

HINT

A good way to tell if a word is a compound is to draw a line between the two smaller parts and ask yourself these questions: Is each smaller part a word? If one of the smaller parts is not a word, the larger word is not a compound. Do the two parts make sense when put together?

Example

Look at the following words. Which words are compound words?

bookcase	sandwich	snowflake	fifteen
costume	message	storeroom	butterfly
automatic	homemade		

_____

_____

Which words are not compound words?

_____

_____

Structural Analysis: Recognizing Prefixes, Suffixes, and Roots

Remember

Prefixes and meanings:

dis	not
in/im	not
mis	wrong
over	too much
pre	before
re	back/again
un	opposite of

Suffixes and meanings:

able	can be
er/or	one who
ful	full of
ish	like
less	without
ment	state of being
ness	state of

Roots and meanings:

dict	say
duct	take/lead
graph	write
ject	throw/force
port	carry
pos	put/place
scribe	write
spect	look/watch

Prefixes A prefix is a word part that is added to the **beginning** of a word. Adding a prefix changes the meaning of a word. For example, the prefix pre means "before." When the prefix pre is added to the word paid, a new word is created. That word is prepaid. Prepaid means "paid before."

Suffixes A suffix is a word part that is added to the **end** of a word. Adding a suffix changes the meaning of a word. For example, the suffix ful means "full of." When the suffix ful is added to the word faith, a new word is created. That word is faithful. Faithful means "full of faith."

Roots A root is the **main word part** to which a prefix or suffix can be added. Knowing the meaning of roots will help you define words. The root in the word spectator, for example, is spect. Spect has something to do with looking or watching. Spectator, therefore, means "someone who watches."

Example

Use the lists in the **Remember** Box to determine the meaning of these words: retell, misspell, foolish, conductor, project, and predict.

_____

_____

_____

_____

_____

_____

_____

Phonetic Analysis: Recognizing Consonant and Vowel Sounds

Consonant Sounds Certain consonants, like the letters c and g, have two sounds.

The letter c can have either a soft or hard sound. It has a soft sound when it has the sound of s, like in the word face. It has a hard sound when it has the sound of k, like in the word calendar.

The letter g can also have a soft or hard sound. It has a soft sound when it has the sound of j, like in the word giraffe. It has a hard sound in the word gorilla.

Single Vowel Sounds A single vowel often has either a short or long sound.

Short a sounds like the a in flag. Long a sounds like the a in frame.

Short e sounds like the e in elf. Long e sounds like the e in decide.

Short i sounds like the i in wink. Long i sounds like the i in island.

Short o sounds like the o in copy. Long o sounds like the o in note.

Short a sounds like the u in unless. Long u sounds like the u in ruler.

Double Vowel Sounds In some words, two vowels stand for one sound.

ee, ei = long e	green, seize
ei = long a	eight
ea = long e	lean
ea = short e	bread

> **HINT**
>
> Say a word out loud a few times to make sure you hear the consonant and vowel sounds.

SKILL FOCUS

ie = long e or i   shield, tried

oa, ow, oe = long o   roast, shadow, tomatoes

Special Vowel Sounds Here are some more vowel pairs and words that show their sounds.

oo = moon

au, aw = taught, claws

ew = few

ui = suit

Example

Which word has the same sound as the ea in treasure?

    defeat   heard   ahead

_____

Which word has the same sound as the o in vote?

    cold   movie   mother

_____

Which word has the same sound as the g in getting?

    imagine   germ   fig

_____

Word Study Skills

DIRECTIONS ▶

In each question, there are three words. Decide which word is a compound word. Then mark the space for the answer you have chosen.

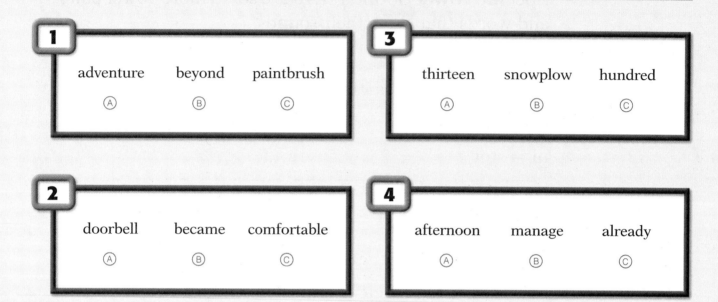

1

adventure   beyond   paintbrush

Ⓐ   Ⓑ   Ⓒ

3

thirteen   snowplow   hundred

Ⓐ   Ⓑ   Ⓒ

2

doorbell   became   comfortable

Ⓐ   Ⓑ   Ⓒ

4

afternoon   manage   already

Ⓐ   Ⓑ   Ⓒ

DIRECTIONS ▶

Read each question and choose the correct answer. Then mark the space for the answer you have chosen.

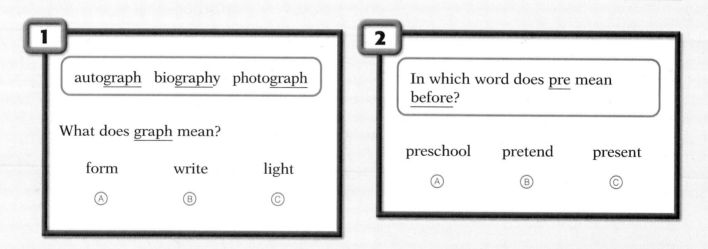

1

autograph   biography   photograph

What does graph mean?

form   write   light

Ⓐ   Ⓑ   Ⓒ

2

In which word does pre mean before?

preschool   pretend   present

Ⓐ   Ⓑ   Ⓒ

3

In the word <u>disappointment</u>, <u>ment</u> probably means —

without   state of   able to

Ⓐ   Ⓑ   Ⓒ

4

In which word does <u>im</u> mean <u>not</u>?

imagine   important   impossible

Ⓐ   Ⓑ   Ⓒ

DIRECTIONS ▶

Look at the word with the underlined letter or letters. The underlined letter or letters stand for a sound. Decide which of the other three words has the same sound in it. Then mark the space for the answer you have chosen.

1

pl<u>ea</u>sant

repeat   beard   head

Ⓐ   Ⓑ   Ⓒ

3

<u>g</u>ather

magic   gem   signal

Ⓐ   Ⓑ   Ⓒ

2

<u>wr</u>ote

sold   model   bother

Ⓐ   Ⓑ   Ⓒ

4

m<u>ea</u>dow

search   weather   season

Ⓐ   Ⓑ   Ⓒ

Reading Vocabulary

Recognizing Synonyms

Sometimes two words have the same, or nearly the same, meaning. These words are called *synonyms*. You can usually find a synonym by putting the word in a sentence. Then take the word out of the sentence and leave a blank. Find a word that fits in the blank so the sentence makes sense.

Keep in mind that you can only replace a noun with a noun, a verb with a verb, and so on. A synonym will always be the same part of speech as the original word.

Determining Correct Choices Suppose you are given this sentence: My mother might <u>permit</u> me to leave if I finish my chores. You are given four possible synonyms for <u>permit</u>: A, <u>agree</u>; B, <u>insist</u>; C, <u>allow</u>; or D, <u>force</u>. Replace the word <u>permit</u> with one of the choices. Which one makes sense?

Neither Choice A, <u>agree</u>, nor Choice B, <u>insist</u>, makes sense in the sentence. Choice D, <u>force</u>, would fit into the sentence, but it does not make sense that a child would be forced to leave. Choice C, "My mother might <u>allow</u> me to leave if I finish my chores" does make sense. The words <u>allow</u> and <u>permit</u> mean the same thing. They are synonyms.

Now use this method to find a synonym for the word <u>center</u>.

> ### HINT
>
> A *synonym* means the same or nearly the same as another word, and it is also the same part of speech.

Example

     My house is in the <u>center</u> of the street.

Your choices are A, <u>north</u>; B, <u>middle</u>; C, <u>name</u>; or D, <u>line</u>. Try each of the choices in the sentence.
Which answer makes sense? Why does it make sense?

_____

_____

_____

Understanding Multiple-Meaning Words

Many words can have more than one meaning. Sometimes this is because a word can be used as both a noun (a person, place, thing, or idea), a verb (an action or state of being), or a modifier. For example: The word <u>play</u> is used as a *noun* when it means "a show on a stage." The word <u>play</u> is used as a *verb* when you <u>play</u> a game.

Sometimes words can have different meanings even when the part of speech is the same. For example, the noun <u>file</u> can mean "a folder," "a tool," or "a line."

Determining Correct Choices Read this sentence: "My room did not contain one speck of <u>dust</u>." The word <u>dust</u> is a noun, meaning "dirt."

What does the word <u>dust</u> mean in this sentence? "It is my job to <u>dust</u> the tables." In this sentence, <u>dust</u> is a verb, something you do. It means "to clean."

> ### HINT
>
> The word <u>multiple</u> means "more than one."

Example

Read the following sentence. Ricky likes to <u>rest</u> before dinner.

In which sentence does the word <u>rest</u> mean the same thing as in the sentence above? How did you arrive at the answer?

A I like this book better than the <u>rest</u>.
B We stopped for a short <u>rest</u>.
C The car came to <u>rest</u> at the corner.
D My mother wanted to <u>rest</u> on the airplane.

_____

_____

_____

Analyzing Context Clues

You can often learn the meaning of a word you do not know if you read it in a sentence. This is because you understand what the sentence is trying to tell you. Sentences often contain clues or hints that help you understand what the word means.

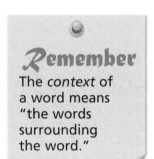

Remember
The *context* of a word means "the words surrounding the word."

If you understand what a sentence is trying to tell you, you can learn the meaning of a word you do not know through its context. This means that you can use the setting of a word in a sentence to learn what the word means.

You use the words you do know in a sentence to understand what the sentence is trying to tell you. You can also use the words you do know in a sentence to help you understand what a word you do not know means.

Determining Correct Choices Suppose you don't know the meaning of the word <u>blend</u> in the following sentence.

You can <u>blend</u> the colors yellow and red to make orange.

You probably know what this sentence is telling you because you understand the words <u>colors</u> and <u>make</u>. This sentence is trying to tell that by mixing two colors together, you can get another color.

From the context of the sentence, it is clear that the word <u>blend</u> means "mix together."

An Extra Example Here is another example. As you read the sentence, use the other words in the sentence to help you figure out what <u>distraught</u> means.

My sister was <u>distraught</u> until her cat found its way home.

Does <u>distraught</u> mean A, <u>excited</u>; B, <u>upset</u>; C, <u>friendly</u>; or D, <u>confused</u>?

The fact that the cat had to find its way home indicates that it was missing. How do most people feel if a pet is missing? From the context of the sentence, it is clear that <u>distraught</u> means B, <u>upset</u>.

Additional Tips If you have trouble answering a question, try these tips:

- Read all the choices first.

- Cross out the choices you know are wrong.

- If you crossed out only one or two choices, go back to the sentence.

- Reread the sentence, looking for clues to the meaning of the underlined word.

Example

Read the following sentence.

With so much talent, the volleyball team expects to <u>dominate</u> the conference this year.

Does <u>dominate</u> mean A, <u>amuse</u>; B, <u>honor</u>; C, <u>signal</u>; or D, <u>control</u>? What clues in the sentence help you find the answer?

_____

_____

_____

_____

Reading Vocabulary

DIRECTIONS ▶

Choose the word or group of words that means the same, or about the same, as the underlined word. Then mark the space for the answer you have chosen.

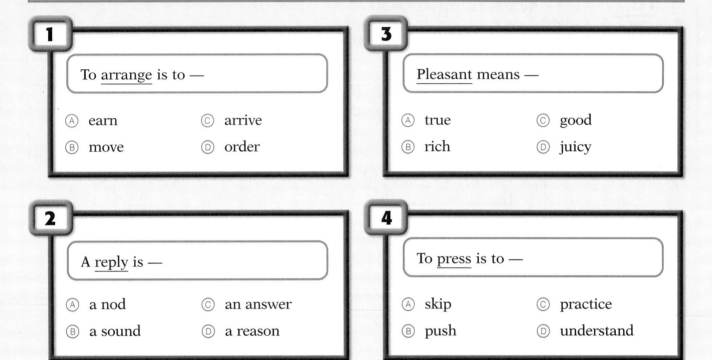

1

To arrange is to —

Ⓐ earn   Ⓒ arrive

Ⓑ move   Ⓓ order

3

Pleasant means —

Ⓐ true   Ⓒ good

Ⓑ rich   Ⓓ juicy

2

A reply is —

Ⓐ a nod   Ⓒ an answer

Ⓑ a sound   Ⓓ a reason

4

To press is to —

Ⓐ skip   Ⓒ practice

Ⓑ push   Ⓓ understand

DIRECTIONS ▶

Read the sentence in the box. Then choose the answer in which the underlined word is used in the same way. Mark the space for the answer you have chosen.

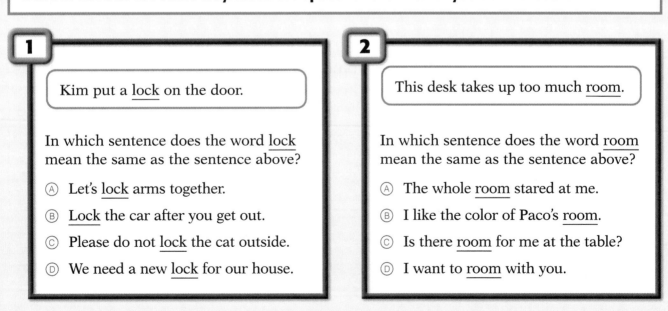

1

Kim put a lock on the door.

In which sentence does the word lock mean the same as the sentence above?

Ⓐ Let's lock arms together.

Ⓑ Lock the car after you get out.

Ⓒ Please do not lock the cat outside.

Ⓓ We need a new lock for our house.

2

This desk takes up too much room.

In which sentence does the word room mean the same as the sentence above?

Ⓐ The whole room stared at me.

Ⓑ I like the color of Paco's room.

Ⓒ Is there room for me at the table?

Ⓓ I want to room with you.

3

Can you carry that <u>load</u> of wood?

In which sentence does the word <u>load</u> mean the same as the sentence above?

Ⓐ That is a heavy <u>load</u> of hay.

Ⓑ Do not <u>load</u> your plate with cookies.

Ⓒ My father washed a <u>load</u> of clothes.

Ⓓ Please <u>load</u> the car for our trip.

4

I did not like that <u>part</u> of the story.

In which sentence does the word <u>part</u> mean the same as the sentence above?

Ⓐ I like to <u>part</u> my hair on the side.

Ⓑ She had the best <u>part</u> in the play.

Ⓒ We have to <u>part</u> at noon.

Ⓓ Which <u>part</u> of the book do you like?

DIRECTIONS ▶

As you read each sentence, use the other words in the sentence to help you figure out what the underlined word means. Then mark the space for the answer you have chosen.

1

The children were very <u>calm</u> during nap time. <u>Calm</u> means —

Ⓐ neat   Ⓒ weak

Ⓑ kind   Ⓓ quiet

3

We heard a <u>faint</u> sound coming from the room. <u>Faint</u> means —

Ⓐ dry   Ⓒ plain

Ⓑ soft   Ⓓ blind

2

We did not know how our new puppy would <u>behave</u>. <u>Behave</u> means —

Ⓐ act   Ⓒ know

Ⓑ drift   Ⓓ depend

4

Kristen <u>chuckled</u> at the funny joke. <u>Chuckled</u> means —

Ⓐ cried   Ⓒ fought

Ⓑ cared   Ⓓ laughed

Literary Reading Comprehension

Determining Supporting Details

Supporting details are bits of information that help tell a story. To find supporting details use the **Hint**.

Example

Read this passage.

Back in the Game

Louisa carefully tied and double-knotted her shoestrings. She had not played soccer since she sprained her ankle.

That day, the coach helped her off the field. The nurse wrapped Louisa's ankle. The doctor said that nothing was broken but she must not play soccer for two weeks.

Today, Louisa would play again. Her team was counting on her. Her heart thumped extra hard. Her hands trembled. She took three deep breaths before she ran onto the field.

Read this information to help you answer the question at the end of the page.

Think about the two questions in the **Hint**. The author tells about Louisa's injury and gives supporting details about it.

What details tell about Louisa's injured ankle?

_____

_____

_____

Providing Support for Conclusions

A *conclusion* is what you decide after you read a story. Look at details from "Back in the Game" on page 48 to see if you know enough to draw a conclusion about the story.

If somebody asked you to explain your conclusion about a passage, you would use facts and details from the passage to support what you have decided.

Remember

Provide means to give.

A *conclusion* is what you decide after you read a story.

Support is made up of the details that back up what you have decided.

Read this information to help you answer the question at the end of the page.

Drawing Conclusions The author never says Louisa was sad or worried. The author does use details to help you decide for yourself how Louisa feels at the end of the story.

Reread "Back in the Game" on page 48. Look at how Louisa is described at the end of the story.

Supporting Conclusions What details did you find that show how Louisa feels? [You probably found three details. "Her heart thumped extra hard. Her hands trembled. She took three deep breaths before she ran onto the field."]

What is your conclusion about how Louisa feels?

_____

_____

_____

_____

Determining Problems and Solutions in Text

A *problem* is something that needs to be fixed. In a story, a problem might be two friends arguing, some sad news, or a lost pet. A *solution* is the way a problem gets fixed.

HINT

Determine means "to find or figure out."

A *problem* is something that needs to be fixed.

A *solution* is the way a problem gets fixed.

Example

Read this passage.

Lost Cat

The skinny, gray kitten shivered on our porch. It was covered with grass and leaves.

"Mom!" I shouted. "There's a lost kitten out here. It just ran under the rosebush."

"First, we must see if it's healthy and if it has a home," Mom said.

We took it to the vet. Then we put posters all around the block. We checked with the animal shelter. After a week, the kitten was still with us.

"Now can we keep it?" I begged.

"Okay, Ty," agreed my mom. "What shall we call him?"

I thought for a moment. "He hid in the rosebush, so let's name him Bushy."

"I like it," my mom said as she hugged me and Bushy.

Read this information to help you answer the question at the end of the page.

Problem: The family must make a plan for the kitten.

How do Ty and Mom finally solve the problem?

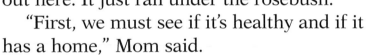

_____

_____

SKILL FOCUS

Determining Author's Intended Audience

An *intended audience* is the readers an author thinks about when writing. The author wants to be sure those people understand what is being said.

Have you ever read a book or watched something on television that seemed to be made just for you? You may have been part of somebody's intended audience.

Read this information to help you answer the question at the end of the page.

Reread "Lost Cat" on page 50. As you read, ask yourself who would enjoy this story.

Intended Audience You probably decided the audience was made up of animal lovers. If you have had a similar experience, you may have felt the story was written for you.

Character's Actions What clues made you think Ty and his mother love animals? [You probably noticed that Ty cared about the skinny, dirty kitten. Also you probably saw that his mother knew that it should be checked by a vet. She thought about other animal lovers. She realized someone might be looking for a lost kitten.]

Who would like to know what the family did after finding the kitten?

_____

_____

_____

The Daytime Stars

Sun lived in the sky all alone, while his sister Moon had all the stars in the sky shining beside her. Sun was lonely and wanted some of them for himself.

"I will make a deal with you," Sun said to Moon. "I will shine on you every night from the other side of the world and help you light the darkness, and I will help you grow full again each month after you fade away to nothing. But I want you to give me some of your stars. I do not want to shine all by myself."

"You must ask them yourself," said Moon. "They have minds of their own."

So Sun sent a message to the stars on a silver cloud. "Please come and share the day sky with me," his message said. "If you will keep me company, I will keep you warm." Sun waited for many days, but no stars came to visit him. Finally, he grew so lonely and so sad that he hid behind a dark cloud.

Then one day Sun heard a voice. He peeked out from behind a cloud and looked around, but he saw no one.

"Has somebody come to visit?" he asked.

"I am a very bright star shining beside you," said the voice. "All the other stars are with me. We have been here all along."

"Are you hiding behind a cloud?" asked Sun.

"No, you are so much brighter than we are that you outshine us," said the star. "But that is fine, because the night is our time to shine. You shine during the day, and you keep us warm."

"I am glad you are here," the Sun said, and he came out from behind a cloud. "I will never be lonely again."

1

What does Sun do so he will not be lonely?

Ⓐ He asks a silver cloud to visit him.

Ⓑ He asks the stars to visit him.

Ⓒ He goes to visit a silver cloud.

Ⓓ He goes to visit the stars.

3

Who would *most* likely enjoy this story?

Ⓐ Someone who does not like the Moon

Ⓑ Someone who is afraid of the dark

Ⓒ Someone who likes the night sky

Ⓓ Someone who plays outside

2

How do you know that Sun is brighter than Moon?

Ⓐ Moon does not outshine the stars.

Ⓑ Moon keeps all the stars with her.

Ⓒ Sun does not come out at night.

Ⓓ Sun is jealous of Moon.

4

Sun makes a deal with Moon because he is —

Ⓐ angry

Ⓑ hidden

Ⓒ lonely

Ⓓ shining

Informational Reading Comprehension

Distinguishing Important from Less Important Ideas

An idea that is *important* to the passage is something you need to know before you can understand what the author is trying to tell you. An idea that is *less important* to the passage gives extra information, but you may be able to understand the author's message without it.

HINT

To tell the difference between important and less important ideas ask:

What is the author trying to explain?

What information is extra?

Example

Read this passage.

Sleeping Upside Down

Did you know that some animals sleep upside down? Bats sleep hanging from roofs or caves. Bats can sleep upside down because they have claws that work like human hands. Hanging this way helps bats hide while they sleep during the day. Hanging upside down makes for an easy takeoff for flying into the night to hunt for food. Some bats eat fruit, and other bats eat insects.

Read this information to help you answer the question at the end of the page.

Important Ideas List four important facts about bats hanging upside down. [They hang from roofs and caves. They use claws to hang upside down. Hanging helps them hide during the day. Hanging makes takeoff easy.]

One sentence does not help you learn about bats sleeping upside down. Which sentence has less important information?

_____

Analyzing Author's Purpose, Assumptions, or Viewpoint

Authors' reasons, or *purposes*, for writing may be to show they care about something. They want to express their *viewpoint*, or opinion, on something they feel strongly about.

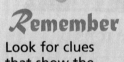

Remember

Look for clues that show the author's feelings or opinion. Words like "we should" or "this is the best" are clues.

Example

Read this passage.

Too Much Light

The sky is full of beautiful night lights. Bright stars come in red and blue and white and yellow. The Milky Way has so many stars that it shines like a river of fresh milk. Most of us will never see the natural light in the night sky. We have too much light coming from the lamps on our streets, and around our stores. How sad it is that we will never see the colors of the stars or the shining light of the Milky Way. We should remember to turn out the lights so we can see the sky.

Read this information to help you answer the question at the end of the page.

Clues Find clues from the passage that show the author feels strongly about seeing the stars. [Words like "how sad" and "turn out the lights so we can see the sky" are clues.]

Viewpoint From these clues, what do you think the author's viewpoint is? [You probably think the author wants to be able to see the stars, so he or she wants fewer lights on Earth.]

What is the author's purpose?

_____

Determining Causes and Effects

Something that happens in a passage is an event. The cause is *why* something happened in the story. The effect is *what* happened as a result of the cause.

Example

Read this passage.

Snow Cones

The first snow cones really were made of snow. People did not know how to make ice, but they knew where to find it. Some people got ice from the tops of snowy mountains. People in Peru cut ice from mountain glaciers. They lowered the ice down the mountains. They used the ice to make snow cones because they were very thirsty. They made snow cones with honey and fruit.

Read this information to help you answer the question at the end of the page.

Event Think about what happened in the passage. [People got thirsty.]

Cause of Event What did being thirsty lead to? [Making snow cones]

What was the effect of people making snow cones?

_____

_____

HINT

If you can answer these two questions, you should be able to set the purpose for reading: What kind of passage is this? What did I learn from reading the passage?

Setting a Purpose

The *purpose* of a passage might be to make the reader laugh or to teach a lesson. Deciding what kind of passage you are reading will help you set a purpose for reading it.

Example

Read this passage.

Smokey Bear

You might not know Smokey Bear, but your parents probably do. Smokey Bear used to be on television. He was a cartoon bear with an important message. The first Smokey Bear was a real bear. He lived in Lincoln National Forest in New Mexico. There was a big fire in the forest. A park ranger found a little bear cub clinging to a tree and named him Smokey Bear. Smokey Bear helped teach people how they could help. Smokey said "Only *You* Can Prevent Wildfires."

Read this information to help you answer the question at the end of the page.

Kind of Passage Ask yourself if this passage is to tell you something or to be fun. (The passage should tell you something.)

What is the purpose of reading "Smokey Bear"?

_____

_____

_____

Making Silk

Most people grow fruit trees because they want ripe, healthy fruit. But did you know that people grow mulberry trees because they want strong, healthy worms? Silkworms feed on the mulberry leaves. These insects work hard to make the silk we use for our clothing.

Humans make silk, too. That is what Mr. Jenkins does. Mr. Jenkins lives where mulberry trees grow well. He buys the trees from a garden shop, and he orders tiny silkworm eggs through the mail.

Mr. Jenkins takes good care of his mulberry trees. He wants strong trees with big leaves. Silkworms love to eat these big leaves. Mr. Jenkins takes good care of his silkworms, too. He keeps the eggs warm in a cardboard box. In about two weeks, the eggs turn into woolly, black worms. He puts the worms on his mulberry trees. The worms eat the leaves and grow healthy and strong.

Strong, healthy silkworms spin strong, healthy cocoons. Silk makers boil these cocoons in soap and water to get the silk. Many silk makers let some of the silk moths out of the cocoons before they boil the cocoons, but most silkworms die in their cocoons.

Mr. Jenkins does not want his silkworms to die, so he makes "peace silk." He frees all of the moths before he boils the cocoons. He lets the moths live out their lives. Then he buys more silkworm eggs to feed on his mulberry trees.

Peace silk is the best kind of silk to have. The silk Mr. Jenkins has is soft. When he has enough silk, he sells it. He uses some of the money to buy more silkworm eggs and more mulberry trees.

1

This passage was written to —

Ⓐ introduce readers to Mr. Jenkins and mulberry trees

Ⓑ entertain readers with a tale about a man and a silkworm

Ⓒ teach students about silkworms

Ⓓ inform readers about the facts of silk production

3

Which of the following statements is the *least important* to know if you want to own silkworms and collect silk?

Ⓐ Silk comes from cocoons.

Ⓑ Peace silk is soft.

Ⓒ Silkworms eat mulberry leaves.

Ⓓ Cocoons are boiled in soap and water.

2

Which of the following sentences expresses Mr. Jenkins' viewpoint?

Ⓐ Silkworms should not die in their cocoons.

Ⓑ People who live in the United States can own silkworms.

Ⓒ Mr. Jenkins buys mulberry trees from a garden shop.

Ⓓ Strong, healthy silkworms make strong, healthy cocoons.

4

What happens when silkworm eggs are placed in cardboard boxes?

Ⓐ The silkworms make cocoons from mulberry leaves.

Ⓑ The silkworms turn into silk moths.

Ⓒ The silkworms eat mulberry leaves.

Ⓓ The silkworms hatch into black, woolly worms.

Functional Reading Comprehension

Forming a Hypothesis

Hypothesis [hi-POTH-uh-sis] is a fancy word for "guess." To find the meaning of the passage, look at the words and pictures.

Remember

To form a *hypothesis*, or a good guess, think of questions you have about what you are reading. Then see whether the answers are in the text. If the answers are not there, make your best guess.

Example

Read the passage.

DELICIOUS Fire-Baked Potatoes for Campers

What you need:

- One large potato for each camper
- Foil for wrapping each potato
- A dinner knife for cutting
- 18-inch wooden sticks
- Salt
- Butter
- Hot coals

What to do:

Choose potatoes. Wash them and pat them dry. Wrap each potato in wrapping foil. Use wooden sticks to cover the potatoes with coals. Bake the potatoes about thirty minutes. Use the wooden sticks to roll the potatoes from underneath the coals. Have an older person cut each potato down the middle. Pull the sides apart. Butter and salt the potato.

Read this information to help you answer the question at the end of the page.

Does the author say to build a campfire?

How can you guess that you need to have a campfire to use this recipe?

_____

Using Graphics

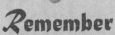

Remember

Graphics usually do not take the place of words, but they help the reader understand. Use both the pictures and words together in a passage to get all the information.

Graphics [GRAF-iks] are pictures or even print styles that can help you understand what you are reading. A picture may show something from the passage to make an idea clear. As you read, look for graphics that will help you understand the information.

Here is a sentence written in three ways. Look carefully at the words in special type. Think about the different ways the sentences can be read.

- The potatoes are great for US.

- The POTATOES are really great.

- The potatoes are really GREAT.

Each sentence has a slightly different meaning.

Read this information to help you answer the question at the end of the page.

Reread "Delicious Fire-Baked Potatoes for Campers." Look for the word that shows how the author feels about the potatoes. [The author calls the potatoes "delicious."]

Special Look See that the way the word *delicious* looks makes you really look at it.

Picture The campfire shows where the potatoes are cooked.

Why does the author call the potatoes "delicious"?

_____

_____

A Note for Lucinda

Dear Lucinda,

Surprise! I hope you had a great day at school. You have been doing a good job keeping your room neat and clean. I left you a little gift because I am so proud of you.

Here are a few things to do when you get home from school:

1. Call me to tell me you are home.
2. Knock on your Dad's office door to tell him where you are. (He's working at home today.)
3. Eat a piece of fruit before you eat anything else.
4. Practice the piano for 30 minutes. (You have a make-up lesson on Friday.)
5. Write a thank-you note to Grandma for the birthday money. We'll mail it later.
6. Start your homework.

Supper is in the slow cooker. If you and Dad will set the table, I can have dinner ready a few minutes after I get home from work.

Then we'll be off to softball practice.

Love,

Mom

1

Who will stay with Lucinda after she gets home?

Ⓐ Her father

Ⓑ Her mother

Ⓒ Her grandmother

Ⓓ Her piano teacher

2

Why did Lucinda's mother say, "You have been doing a good job"?

Ⓐ Lucinda had practiced piano.

Ⓑ Lucinda had done her homework.

Ⓒ Lucinda had helped her Dad.

Ⓓ Lucinda had kept her room nice.

3

Where did Lucinda find the note her mother left?

Ⓐ In the kitchen

Ⓑ On the piano

Ⓒ In her bedroom

Ⓓ In the family room

4

Lucinda's mother *probably* wrote her a note because —

Ⓐ she was leaving for work

Ⓑ she was in the home office

Ⓒ she was out of town that day

Ⓓ Lucinda asked her mother to write her a note

Word Study Skills

DIRECTIONS ▶

In each question, there are three words. Decide which word is a compound word. Then mark the space for the answer you have chosen.

SAMPLE A

center   beyond   tablecloth
Ⓐ   Ⓑ   Ⓒ

1

husband   doghouse   forgotten
Ⓐ   Ⓑ   Ⓒ

2

rainstorm   chocolate   vegetable
Ⓐ   Ⓑ   Ⓒ

3

bargain   sudden   pancake
Ⓐ   Ⓑ   Ⓒ

4

brighter   sidewalk   fasten
Ⓐ   Ⓑ   Ⓒ

DIRECTIONS ▶

Read each question and choose the best answer. Then mark the space for the answer you have chosen.

SAMPLE B

The <u>un</u> in <u>unlikely</u> means the same as the <u>im</u> in —

imagine   imperfect   improve
Ⓐ   Ⓑ   Ⓒ

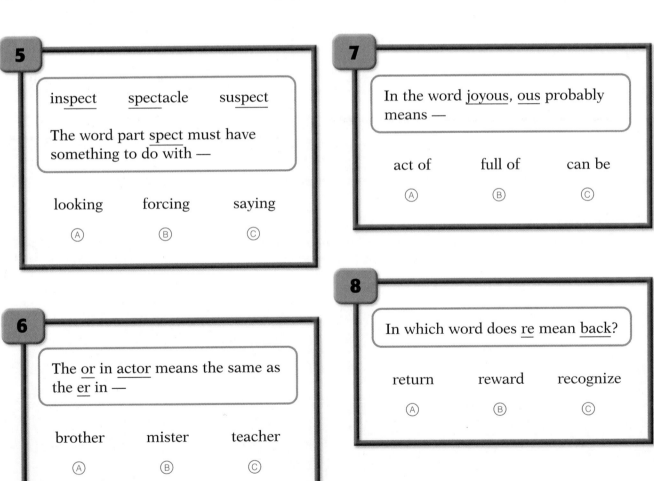

5

inspect   <u>spectacle</u>   suspect

The word part <u>spect</u> must have something to do with —

looking   forcing   saying
Ⓐ   Ⓑ   Ⓒ

7

In the word <u>joyous</u>, <u>ous</u> probably means —

act of   full of   can be
Ⓐ   Ⓑ   Ⓒ

6

The <u>or</u> in <u>actor</u> means the same as the <u>er</u> in —

brother   mister   teacher
Ⓐ   Ⓑ   Ⓒ

8

In which word does <u>re</u> mean <u>back</u>?

return   reward   recognize
Ⓐ   Ⓑ   Ⓒ

9

In which word does <u>un</u> mean <u>not</u>?

unlock   unite   unless

Ⓐ   Ⓑ   Ⓒ

11

In which word does <u>or</u> mean <u>one who</u>?

tractor   sailor   mirror

Ⓐ   Ⓑ   Ⓒ

10

In which word does <u>dis</u> mean <u>not</u>?

disappear   discover   disease

Ⓐ   Ⓑ   Ⓒ

12

In the word <u>oversleep</u>, <u>over</u> probably means—

before   opposite of   too much

Ⓐ   Ⓑ   Ⓒ

DIRECTIONS ▶

Look at the word with the underlined letter or letters. The underlined letter or letters stand for a sound. Decide which of the other three words has the same sound in it. Then mark the space for the answer you have chosen.

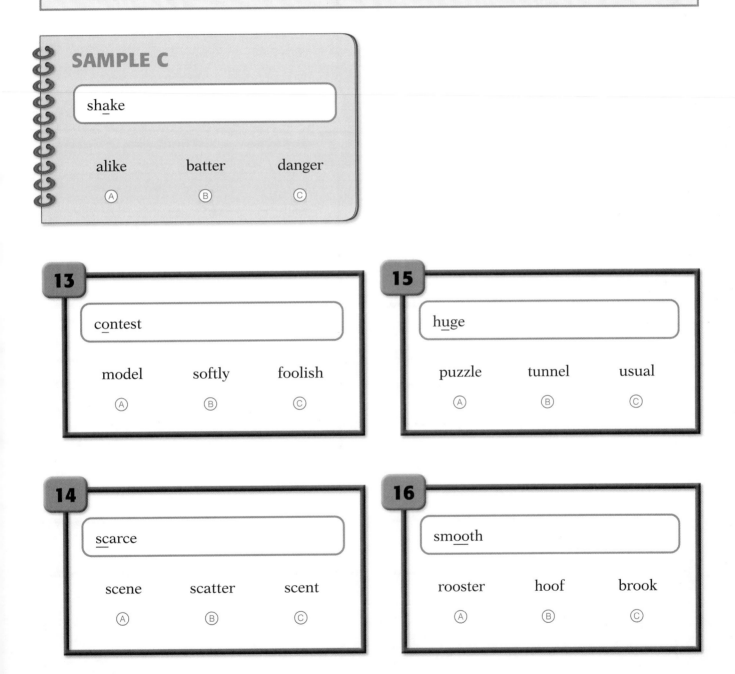

SAMPLE C

sh<u>a</u>ke

alike   batter   danger
ⓐ   ⓑ   ⓒ

13

c<u>o</u>ntest

model   softly   foolish
ⓐ   ⓑ   ⓒ

14

<u>sc</u>arce

scene   scatter   scent
ⓐ   ⓑ   ⓒ

15

h<u>u</u>ge

puzzle   tunnel   usual
ⓐ   ⓑ   ⓒ

16

sm<u>oo</u>th

rooster   hoof   brook
ⓐ   ⓑ   ⓒ

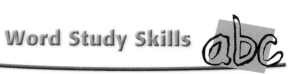

17

div_ide

pitch
Ⓐ

birth
Ⓑ

strike
Ⓒ

21

c_up

butcher
Ⓐ

rush
Ⓑ

tube
Ⓒ

18

_address

rather
Ⓐ

tape
Ⓑ

sale
Ⓒ

22

s_eventy

become
Ⓐ

deserve
Ⓑ

tender
Ⓒ

19

_cellar

cause
Ⓐ

canoe
Ⓑ

center
Ⓒ

23

tr_easure

meal
Ⓐ

fellow
Ⓑ

search
Ⓒ

20

l_onely

woman
Ⓐ

colt
Ⓑ

loft
Ⓒ

24

st_out

crowd
Ⓐ

lower
Ⓑ

borrow
Ⓒ

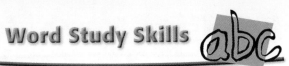

25

neighbor

peek   eight   earth

Ⓐ   Ⓑ   Ⓒ

28

imagine

animal   ripe   pilot

Ⓐ   Ⓑ   Ⓒ

26

bench

metal   hero   become

Ⓐ   Ⓑ   Ⓒ

29

beach

wear   learn   needle

Ⓐ   Ⓑ   Ⓒ

27

tower

although   trousers   arrow

Ⓐ   Ⓑ   Ⓒ

30

bridge

knife   pilot   list

Ⓐ   Ⓑ   Ⓒ

Reading Vocabulary

DIRECTIONS ▶

Choose the word or group of words that mean the same, or about the same, as the underlined word. Then mark the space for the answer you have chosen.

SAMPLE A

To weep is to —

Ⓐ run   Ⓒ cry

Ⓑ laugh   Ⓓ sleep

1

An automobile is a —

Ⓐ car   Ⓒ airplane

Ⓑ train   Ⓓ bicycle

2

A claw is most like a —

Ⓐ foot   Ⓒ beak

Ⓑ nail   Ⓓ feather

3

A speck is a —

Ⓐ glass   Ⓒ spot

Ⓑ stem   Ⓓ bulb

4

Familiar means —

Ⓐ lost   Ⓒ good

Ⓑ known   Ⓓ pretty

5

A <u>captain</u> is most like a —

Ⓐ team   Ⓒ sailor

Ⓑ ship   Ⓓ leader

6

A <u>crumb</u> is a —

Ⓐ chain   Ⓒ bit

Ⓑ plate   Ⓓ slice

7

<u>Healthy</u> means —

Ⓐ main   Ⓒ well

Ⓑ hungry   Ⓓ grand

8

To <u>imagine</u> means to —

Ⓐ dream   Ⓒ allow

Ⓑ blush   Ⓓ chew

9

<u>Bold</u> means —

Ⓐ light   Ⓒ scared

Ⓑ wrong   Ⓓ brave

10

To <u>trust</u> means to —

Ⓐ believe   Ⓒ need

Ⓑ love   Ⓓ hold

11

To <u>steal</u> is to —

Ⓐ hug   Ⓒ rob

Ⓑ slide   Ⓓ land

12

To <u>amaze</u> is to —

Ⓐ amuse   Ⓒ complete

Ⓑ surprise   Ⓓ delight

DIRECTIONS ▶

Read the sentence in the box. Then choose the answer in which the underlined word is used in the same way. Mark the space for the answer you have chosen.

SAMPLE B

> Our house is at the base of the mountain.

In which sentence does the word base mean the same as in the sentence above?

Ⓐ Michael slid into second base.

Ⓑ The tower's base needs painting.

Ⓒ That company set up its main base in St. Louis.

Ⓓ Our friend lives at the army base down the road.

13

> Post your picture on the wall.

In which sentence does the word post mean the same as in the sentence above?

Ⓐ Our teacher will post the grades today.

Ⓑ The horse stood near the starting post.

Ⓒ The bird sat on the fence post near the driveway.

Ⓓ Where is the new post office?

14

> Did Karen iron her pants?

In which sentence does the word iron mean the same as in the sentence above?

Ⓐ The cowboy branded the ranch's cattle with a hot iron.

Ⓑ Rosa didn't iron her shirt.

Ⓒ Please turn off the iron.

Ⓓ Mom's skillet is made of iron.

15

> After 3 games his average bowling score was 100.

In which sentence does the word average mean the same as in the sentence above?

Ⓐ The average movie is an hour long.

Ⓑ I bought an average number of carrots.

Ⓒ The class average was a B on the spelling test.

Ⓓ On an average day, ten people buy the book.

16

My classroom is down the <u>hall</u>.

In which sentence does the word <u>hall</u> mean the same as in the sentence above?

Ⓐ The <u>hall</u> near my office is long.

Ⓑ She spoke at the meeting <u>hall</u>.

Ⓒ The mayor spoke at the town <u>hall</u>.

Ⓓ I ate lunch in the dining <u>hall</u>.

18

Use a <u>model</u> to solve a problem.

In which sentence does the word <u>model</u> mean the same as in the sentence above?

Ⓐ We like to make <u>model</u> airplanes.

Ⓑ Carolyn likes to <u>model</u> clothes.

Ⓒ She taught us how to <u>model</u> clay.

Ⓓ My dad is a good role <u>model</u> for me.

17

My aunt <u>ran</u> a factory for years.

In which sentence does the word <u>ran</u> mean the same as in the sentence above?

Ⓐ Mrs. Hill <u>ran</u> for mayor.

Ⓑ I <u>ran</u> in that race last year.

Ⓒ My mother <u>ran</u> the water in the tub.

Ⓓ My dad <u>ran</u> businesses in two states.

19

The <u>jet</u> was ready to take off.

In which sentence does the word <u>jet</u> mean the same as in the sentence above?

Ⓐ We'll <u>jet</u> to the store before it closes.

Ⓑ A <u>jet</u> of water shot from the pool.

Ⓒ This will be my first time on a <u>jet</u>.

Ⓓ She dyed her hair <u>jet</u> black.

20

The teacher made a <u>mark</u> on the paper to show the student where to look.

In which sentence does the word <u>mark</u> mean the same as in the sentence above?

Ⓐ I made a <u>mark</u> on the box.

Ⓑ I got a high <u>mark</u> on my math test.

Ⓒ He aimed, but he missed the <u>mark</u>.

Ⓓ The trophy was a <u>mark</u> of pride.

21

The <u>patch</u> will cover the hole.

In which sentence does the word <u>patch</u> mean the same as in the sentence above?

Ⓐ Dad has a garden on a <u>patch</u> of land.

Ⓑ The flat tire needs a <u>patch</u>.

Ⓒ I tried to <u>patch</u> the rip in my jeans.

Ⓓ I will <u>patch</u> things up with Mary.

DIRECTIONS ▶

As you read each sentence, use the other words in the sentence to help you figure out what the underlined word means. Then mark the space for the answer you have chosen.

SAMPLE C

He lived on the edge of a steep bluff. Bluff means —

Ⓐ tree   © garden

Ⓑ cliff   Ⓓ valley

24

We left our books in the rain, and they got soaked. Soaked means —

Ⓐ wet   © stacked

Ⓑ read   Ⓓ shelved

22

I felt intelligent when I solved the puzzle by myself. Intelligent means —

Ⓐ bad   © sorry

Ⓑ smart   Ⓓ nervous

25

We hid our money in a secure place where no one could find it. Secure means —

Ⓐ awful   © safe

Ⓑ cozy   Ⓓ quiet

23

My mother was totaling the numbers in her checkbook. Totaling means —

Ⓐ moving   © raising

Ⓑ adding   Ⓓ removing

26

I must tidy my room because I left my toys on the floor. Tidy means —

Ⓐ open   © change

Ⓑ paint   Ⓓ clean

27

The hungry puppy <u>snatched</u> the meat from Juan's hand and ran. <u>Snatched</u> means —

Ⓐ chewed Ⓒ licked

Ⓑ grabbed Ⓓ rubbed

29

The rabbit moved at a quick <u>pace</u>. <u>Pace</u> means —

Ⓐ time Ⓒ moment

Ⓑ speed Ⓓ distance

28

Never dive in <u>shallow</u> water because you might hit your head on a rock. <u>Shallow</u> means —

Ⓐ safe Ⓒ low

Ⓑ clear Ⓓ frozen

30

The <u>infant</u> cried for his mother. <u>Infant</u> means —

Ⓐ player Ⓒ father

Ⓑ neighbor Ⓓ baby

Reading Comprehension

DIRECTIONS ▶

Read each passage. Then read each question about the passage. Decide which is the best answer to the question. Mark the space for the answer you have chosen.

SAMPLES

The Good Bad Habit

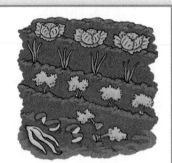

One day Ricky's mother saw him throwing food scraps into the garden. She said, "Ricky, you're a litterbug! Don't you know that ants will come?" Ricky didn't like ants. "And don't you know that worms will come?" his mother said. Ricky kind of liked worms. "Raccoons might come, too," his mother said. "Raccoons might come to eat your food scraps."

Ricky wanted to see raccoons. He watched for them. None came. He looked at the garden. Then he dug into the dirt. He watched the long, healthy earthworms wriggle through the dirt.

Ricky ate a snack in the garden every day. He threw his food scraps into the dirt. He watched the worms wriggle around. The dirt got thicker and richer. Ricky's mother was pleased. "In this case, Ricky, being a litterbug was a good thing. The worms broke down your food scraps and fed the soil. Now we have good, rich compost. It will help our garden grow." Ricky was pleased, too. "I always wanted compost to use in our garden," said Ricky's mother. "I always kind of liked worms!" said Ricky.

A How were worms good for Ricky's garden?

ⓐ They fed the soil.

ⓑ They fed raccoons.

ⓒ They grew big and healthy.

ⓓ They wriggled through the dirt.

B This passage teaches us mainly —

ⓐ how to make a garden

ⓑ how to make compost

ⓒ that Ricky likes worms

ⓓ that Ricky is a litterbug

The Ant and the Grasshopper

Long ago, an ant and a grasshopper lived near one another in a big field. The grasshopper was a cheerful fellow. He spent his days hopping around in the sunshine. The ant was just the opposite. He rarely talked. He never sang. Instead, he worked from sunrise until sunset, carrying kernels of corn and grains of wheat to store inside his anthill.

"Slow down and enjoy yourself!" Grasshopper said. "Ant, you work too hard. We are surrounded by food."

"I have no time to slow down," said Ant. "Squirrel told me it was going to be a very long winter." Ant pointed to Squirrel, who was busy burying nuts. "You should follow our example, Grasshopper. We are storing up food to get us through the long, cold winter."

"You worry too much," said Grasshopper. "Between the farmer's field and his wife's garden, there is always plenty of food for me."

"Do as you please," said Ant. "But don't say I didn't warn you."

Grasshopper shook his head. "There's more to life than work," he said. "You and Squirrel aren't having any fun." Then he left to chirp and play in the sunshine. Grasshopper was too busy playing to notice that the days were getting shorter and the nights were getting cooler. Soon, the leaves fell from the trees. The plants that weren't harvested died and fell to the ground.

One morning, it began to snow and soon snow covered the field. Grasshopper could not find any food.

"Ant!" he called. "Where are you? Please share your food."

Ant stuck his head up from his anthill. "I only have enough for myself," he said. "You should have worked and stored food instead of playing all summer. Now you will have to accept the results of your foolishness."

1

The purpose of this story is to —

Ⓐ persuade the reader to rest

Ⓑ interest the reader in insects

Ⓒ teach the reader a lesson

Ⓓ explain science facts

2

Ant is storing food because —

Ⓐ Squirrel told him a hard winter was coming

Ⓑ Grasshopper will need something to eat

Ⓒ he worries too much

Ⓓ he enjoys working

3

Ant knows that Grasshopper —

Ⓐ will be able to eat the farmer's food

Ⓑ has already stored his own food

Ⓒ will be able to share his food

Ⓓ will not have enough food for winter

4

What conclusion can you draw about Ant and Grasshopper?

Ⓐ They don't like to work.

Ⓑ They are good friends.

Ⓒ Ant plans for the future but Grasshopper doesn't.

Ⓓ Grasshopper stores food but Ant doesn't.

5

This story is written for —

Ⓐ people who work too hard

Ⓑ people who do not work hard

Ⓒ people who like squirrels

Ⓓ people who like insects

6

The last paragraph tells —

Ⓐ why Ant stores his food

Ⓑ the reason Ant is angry

Ⓒ the lesson that Grasshopper learns

Ⓓ why Grasshopper lives in the field

Desert Monsters

Did you know there are monsters in the United States? Lizards called Gila (HE-luh) monsters live in the Arizona desert. What makes Gila monsters special is their bite. Gila monsters have a poison called venom. The poison can kill other animals.

Body

Gila monsters are pink with black and yellow spots. Their tails have black rings. The skin on their head and back is bumpy. Their bellies have smooth scales. They can weigh up to three pounds. They can grow twenty-four inches long.

Homes

Gila monsters like to live in holes in the ground. The desert is hot, and they like to be cool. It is cool deep under the ground.

Food

Gila monsters eat the eggs of small animals, frogs, bugs, and birds, as well as the animals themselves. Gila monsters flick their tongue to smell animals. When they reach the animal, they jump quickly at it and bite it.

Young Gila Monsters

Mother Gila monsters dig holes for their eggs. They cover the eggs with sand. The sun heats the sand, and the sand heats the eggs. The eggs hatch in about four months.

Bites

Gila monsters do not often bite people. Gila monsters will bite, though, if they feel frightened about something. Once they use their special bite, they hold on and chew the animal they are holding. Sometimes Gila monsters will not let go! If you ever see Gila monsters, do not touch them. They are interesting to look at but dangerous to touch.

7

What happens first after a mother Gila monster lays eggs?

Ⓐ The mother digs holes.

Ⓑ The sun heats the sand near the eggs.

Ⓒ The mother covers the eggs with sand.

Ⓓ The sand heats the eggs.

8

What is the *most* important idea in the first paragraph?

Ⓐ Gila monsters are special because of their bite.

Ⓑ There are monsters in the United States.

Ⓒ Gila monsters have a special tail.

Ⓓ Poison can kill animals.

9

To which section of the passage would information about safety *most* likely be added?

Ⓐ Body   Ⓒ Food

Ⓑ Homes   Ⓓ Bites

10

The *main* idea of the third paragraph is that Gila monsters —

Ⓐ like to dig holes

Ⓑ like to live under the ground

Ⓒ steal other animals' homes

Ⓓ like the hot, dry weather

11

Gila monsters chew the animals they bite because —

Ⓐ they like the taste of other animals

Ⓑ they are looking for their eggs

Ⓒ the poison comes out as Gila monsters chew

Ⓓ they can smell the animal when chewing

12

The author wrote the passage to —

Ⓐ persuade readers to raise Gila monsters

Ⓑ inform readers about an interesting lizard

Ⓒ entertain readers with a lizard story

Ⓓ explain how to tame a Gila monster

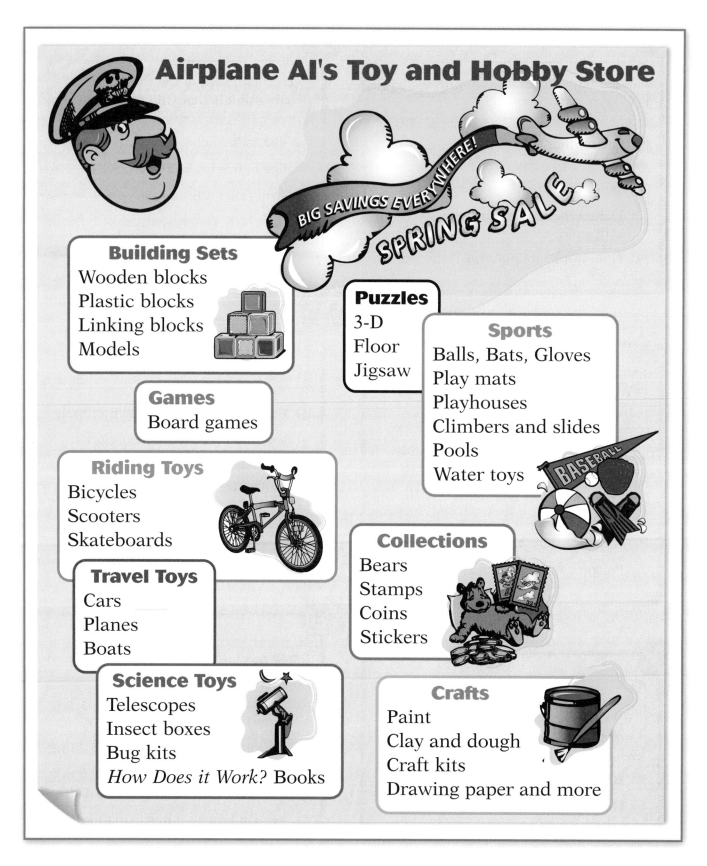

Airplane Al's Toy and Hobby Store

BIG SAVINGS EVERYWHERE!

SPRING SALE

Building Sets
Wooden blocks
Plastic blocks
Linking blocks
Models

Puzzles
3-D
Floor
Jigsaw

Sports
Balls, Bats, Gloves
Play mats
Playhouses
Climbers and slides
Pools
Water toys

Games
Board games

Riding Toys
Bicycles
Scooters
Skateboards

Travel Toys
Cars
Planes
Boats

Collections
Bears
Stamps
Coins
Stickers

Science Toys
Telescopes
Insect boxes
Bug kits
How Does it Work? Books

Crafts
Paint
Clay and dough
Craft kits
Drawing paper and more

13

Based on this ad, which of the following toys would be with the building sets?

Ⓐ Water toys   Ⓒ Stamps

Ⓑ Cars   Ⓓ Models

16

Based on the ad, Airplane Al's *probably* has —

Ⓐ live fish   Ⓒ garden tools

Ⓑ basketballs   Ⓓ schoolbooks

14

In this ad, toys are arranged by —

Ⓐ what size they are

Ⓑ how they are used

Ⓒ what color they are

Ⓓ how much they cost

17

Based on this ad, the author shows that Airplane Al's store has —

Ⓐ hobby supplies for school-age children only

Ⓑ toys and hobby supplies for children

Ⓒ toys and hobby supplies for girls

Ⓓ toys for babies only

15

Based on this ad, you know that —

Ⓐ Airplane Al is a pilot with a toy store

Ⓑ Airplane Al is a man who flies planes

Ⓒ Airplane Al's store has the latest toys

Ⓓ Airplane Al's store is having a sale

18

What do the pictures of toys on the ad explain?

Ⓐ The reason for the ad

Ⓑ The name of Airplane Al

Ⓒ The words in the boxes

Ⓓ The words in the banner

The Butterfly Bus

"Time to wake up," Mother called to Mandy from downstairs. "Time to get ready to catch the Butterfly Bus."

It was Mandy's first day at her new school, and she was a little anxious. She sprang out of bed and put on the pants and shirt she had set out the night before. Then she grabbed her new backpack—the one with the bright colors.

"Hurry up, Mandy," her mother called from the kitchen. "You haven't eaten yet, and the Butterfly Bus will be here any minute."

"What's for breakfast?" Mandy called down the stairs.

"A tower of smiley-face pancakes," her mother called back.

Mandy knew that her mother was trying to help her relax on the first day of school. When she passed by the living room, she saw Frederick, her fish, and noticed that she had forgotten to clean his bowl. *I'll have to clean it after school,* Mandy thought to herself. Then she got an idea. She *rummaged* through the hall closet and found the box with Frederick's food and net. Then she walked into the kitchen.

"Hi, Mom. I'm ready for school," Mandy said with a smile. Her mother looked up from the stove.

"Mandy, I don't think you have time to clean Frederick's bowl now," her mother said. "You'll have to do it after school."

"Oh, I'm not going to clean Frederick's bowl," Mandy said. "I'm going to catch the Butterfly Bus!"

Mandy knew that the Butterfly Bus was really just a school bus with a picture on it, but she wanted to make her mother happy. Her mother laughed. Mandy felt much less nervous about going to school now, and she knew that the picture of the butterfly would help her find the right bus when it was time to come home.

19

What would you look for to find what a character *said*?

Ⓐ Paragraphs

Ⓑ Sentences

Ⓒ Exclamation points

Ⓓ Quotation marks

22

Which of these do Mandy and her mother share?

Ⓐ An exciting bus ride

Ⓑ A funny laugh

Ⓒ A sense of humor

Ⓓ A fish for a pet

20

What made Mandy think of a way to make her mother laugh?

Ⓐ She found the fish net.

Ⓑ She heard the Butterfly Bus.

Ⓒ She saw Frederick's bowl.

Ⓓ She heard what was for breakfast.

23

What makes the Butterfly Bus a short story?

Ⓐ It makes you laugh.

Ⓑ It gives you only facts.

Ⓒ It takes place in the past.

Ⓓ It has make-believe characters.

21

What is the author *mainly* trying to tell you?

Ⓐ That buses take you to school

Ⓑ That laughing helps you relax

Ⓒ That Mandy has chores

Ⓓ That Mandy's mother is busy

24

In this story, the word *rummaged* means —

Ⓐ looked through

Ⓑ opened up

Ⓒ cleaned out

Ⓓ ran around

Bike Riding Is Best

Many students walk to school, and some ride in cars. Only a few students ride bikes to school. This needs to change! Biking to school is best!

Riding a bike does not cost money. Cars need gas, and gas costs money. Parents and families don't like to spend too much money. If students ride bikes to school, their parents and families can save money on gas.

Riding a bike is faster than walking to school. Students often sleep late. They rush through breakfast and then try to run like frightened deer to school. If students rode bikes, they would not be late for school. They could pedal a bike faster than they could ever run. They would leave the walkers behind.

Riding a bike is also great for keeping in shape. It is important to keep in shape. Biking makes your heart beat faster and makes you take deeper breaths. This helps your body grow strong. Biking builds muscle and burns fat. Biking keeps your body fit. Students who ride bikes to school do better in gym class because their bodies are so fit.

Riding a bike is also fun. Healthy minds cannot think about work all the time. Students work hard in school, and they need to have fun during the day. Biking to school is an enjoyable activity that they can do with friends. While racing to school, bikers forget about work for a while.

If you're planning how to get to school, think about riding a bike. Your mind, your body, and your parents' wallets will be glad you did.

25

To find information about the cost of biking, the reader should —

Ⓐ read the title

Ⓑ skim the conclusion

Ⓒ scan the text for key words

Ⓓ look for words in dark type

26

In this passage, what is the effect of a fast heartbeat and deep breaths?

Ⓐ Students have healthy minds.

Ⓑ Students can outrun walkers.

Ⓒ Students take more gym classes.

Ⓓ Students build muscle and burn fat.

27

What can you conclude from reading the passage?

Ⓐ The author cannot ride a bike.

Ⓑ The author likes to ride bikes.

Ⓒ The author walks to school.

Ⓓ The author is unhealthy.

28

The passage states that students who walk to school sometimes "run like frightened deer." This means students are —

Ⓐ breathing hard

Ⓑ walking slowly

Ⓒ moving stiffly

Ⓓ running quickly

29

Where did the author *most likely* get the information in the second paragraph?

Ⓐ From parents or families who own cars

Ⓑ From a book about car repair

Ⓒ From a book about the first cars

Ⓓ From gas station workers

30

What is the main idea of the passage?

Ⓐ It is good to be healthy.

Ⓑ Biking to school saves money.

Ⓒ Students should wake up on time.

Ⓓ Riding a bike is a good idea.

What's Cooking?

Los Altos Elementary Lunch Menu: March 4 through March 8

Monday, March 4
Hamburger OR Chef's Salad with Crackers
Seasoned Potatoes
Fresh Fruit
Trail Mix

Tuesday, March 5
Cheese Nachos OR Oven-Baked Chicken w/Roll
Mini Corn on the Cob
Cucumber and Tomato Salad
Pudding Cup

Wednesday, March 6
Cheese Pizza OR Cook's Choice
Seasoned Green Beans
Salad Mix
Chilled Fruit

Thursday, March 7
Sloppy Joe w/Roll OR Toasted Cheese Sandwich
Chicken Noodle Soup
One Half Dill Pickle
Fruit Fluff with Gelatin

Friday, March 8
Macaroni & Cheese w/Roll OR Taco Salad Bowl
Baked Beans
Baby Carrots & Broccoli
Rosy Applesauce

Lunch Prices:
Lunch $2.00
Extra Milk $ .50

Single Items:
Corn Dog $.50
Hot Dog $.50
Veggie Salad $1.00
Taco Salad $1.00
Chicken Bits $1.50
Yogurt Cup $.50

31

Based on the menu, how much will lunch cost next week?

Ⓐ $.50   Ⓒ $1.50

Ⓑ $1.00   Ⓓ $2.00

32

On which day can a student purchase fresh fruit?

Ⓐ Monday   Ⓒ Wednesday

Ⓑ Tuesday   Ⓓ Thursday

33

What else besides the dates shows that these lunches are for the month of March?

Ⓐ The pictures on the menu

Ⓑ The cost of the single items on the menu

Ⓒ The artwork around the outside of the menu

Ⓓ The name of the school at the top of the menu

34

The purpose of this menu is to tell the —

Ⓐ parents the cost of lunch

Ⓑ teachers the time lunch is served

Ⓒ students which foods are served

Ⓓ cooks which foods should be made

35

"Rosy Applesauce" is a food that is probably colored —

Ⓐ brown   Ⓒ orange

Ⓑ pink   Ⓓ gray

36

"Mini Corn" on the menu means that the corn is —

Ⓐ cut in big pieces

Ⓑ cut off the cob

Ⓒ bigger than normal

Ⓓ smaller than normal

My Alarm Clock

Duke is my alarm clock.

Three barks mean

Get up! Get up! Get up!

Then he wags his tail

And jumps on my bed.

Duke is determined.

He doesn't give up.

He licks my face until I wake up.

Get up! he barks one last time.

I always do what Duke says.

37

What is the last thing Duke does to wake up his owner?

Ⓐ Barks three times

Ⓑ Jumps on the bed

Ⓒ Barks once

Ⓓ Licks the boy's face

40

You know this is a poem because —

Ⓐ the lines rhyme

Ⓑ it has characters

Ⓒ it is very short

Ⓓ it is written in verses

38

After Duke barks the boy will *most likely* —

Ⓐ go back to sleep

Ⓑ get out of bed

Ⓒ tell Duke to go away

Ⓓ go to another room to sleep

41

This poem is written for people who —

Ⓐ don't have pets

Ⓑ own alarm clocks

Ⓒ don't like to sleep

Ⓓ like dogs

39

In the poem, what tells you that Duke is a dog?

Ⓐ Duke is my alarm clock.

Ⓑ Three barks mean Get up!

Ⓒ He doesn't give up.

Ⓓ I always do what Duke says.

42

The first three lines of the poem tell you —

Ⓐ Duke wakes up first

Ⓑ the boy is dreaming

Ⓒ the boy is awake

Ⓓ Duke can talk

The Big Wheel

What is large, round, and carries people high in the sky at a fair? You might have ridden a Ferris Wheel. Have you ever wondered about the first Ferris Wheel?

A Man Named George

In 1890, the leaders of America decided to hold a fair in Chicago, Illinois. American leaders needed something to make this fair special. The leaders held a meeting and talked about ideas. At that time, a young man named George Ferris had a plan for something special. George was a bridge builder. He had learned about steel. Steel was new in 1890, and George was testing it. George wanted to build something from steel for the fair. He thought he had an idea.

Building the Wheel

In 1893, George told the leaders his idea for a large wheel that would carry riders high in the sky. The leaders thought George's idea was crazy. They didn't think a wheel this large could be built. George told them he could do it. The leaders decided to let him try.

George worked for four months to make the wheel. He had to hire many workers and use many pounds of steel to finish the job. When the wheel was finished, it was 264 feet high. It had 36 wooden cars that held 60 people. Each car had a table for people to eat food they brought on the car.

Riding the Wheel

On June 21, 1893, people rode the Ferris Wheel for the first time. Some people were afraid the cars would fall off the wheel. The wheel moved, and the engine growled like a bear. The cars rose higher. People looked out the windows and could see for miles. They laughed and cheered. The Ferris Wheel was a big success!

43

What would be the purpose for reading the passage?

Ⓐ To learn how to build a Ferris Wheel

Ⓑ To enjoy a story about Chicago

Ⓒ To learn about the first Ferris Wheel

Ⓓ To find out about the rides at fairs

44

Which detail shows that the first riders liked the Ferris Wheel?

Ⓐ They were afraid to get on the ride.

Ⓑ They cheered as the cars rose.

Ⓒ They were surprised that they could eat on the cars.

Ⓓ They liked to hear the roar of the engine.

45

In which paragraph would information about the number of people who rode the wheel at the fair *best* fit?

Ⓐ The second paragraph

Ⓑ The third paragraph

Ⓒ The fourth paragraph

Ⓓ The last paragraph

46

What is the *most* important idea in the second paragraph?

Ⓐ American leaders needed something to make this fair special.

Ⓑ The leaders held a meeting and talked about ideas.

Ⓒ George was a bridge builder who knew about using steel.

Ⓓ Steel is a metal used to make bridges and buildings.

47

From the passage, the reader can tell that George —

Ⓐ often attended fairs

Ⓑ easily won the leaders over

Ⓒ wanted to make something new

Ⓓ had never built anything before

48

An engine is compared to a bear because —

Ⓐ the engine sounds like a bear

Ⓑ the engine looks like a bear

Ⓒ the engine is as big as a bear

Ⓓ engines and bears are both unusual

 # WILDLIFE ADVENTURE PARK

Come and see—

TIGERS	ELEPHANTS	SNAKES	MONKEYS
ANTELOPE	LIONS	BUFFALO	LEOPARDS

And many other animals!

It's not a zoo! It's not a circus! Wildlife Adventure Park is like a garden where you can see animals from all over the world. Stay in your car as you drive through the park. Nine different programs each day. See the animals walk or run—just as they would in the wild. Guided tours for school groups.

PARK HOURS

Winter: September through May
9:30 A.M. - 5:00 P.M.
Open Tuesday through Sunday

Summer: June through August
Wed.-Fri. 4:00 P.M. - 9:30 P.M.
Saturday 9:30 A.M. - 9:30 P.M.
Sunday 9:30 A.M. - 5 P.M.

PRICE
General Admission—
Adult - $10.00
Seniors - $8.00
Children - $6.00
Ask about our special group rates.

DO NOT FEED THE ANIMALS.

For general information, call 1-800-555-ANML
Or write: 1400 N. Wild Prairie, Manhattan, Kansas 66502

49

Wildlife Adventure Park is located in —

(A) Prairie, Africa

(B) Manhattan, Kansas

(C) Manhattan, New York

(D) Prairie, Kansas

50

Based on the poster, which animal could you expect to see at the park?

(A) Penguins   (C) Tigers

(B) Fish   (D) Dogs

51

At Wildlife Adventure Park, you can see the animals —

(A) in cages

(B) from cars

(C) in caves

(D) inside buildings

52

If you get out of your car in the Wildlife Adventure Park, the wild animals *probably* will —

(A) hurt you

(B) lick you

(C) eat from your hand

(D) gather around the car

53

Based on the poster, the author thinks that some animals are better off living —

(A) on a farm   (C) behind bars

(B) in a zoo   (D) in the wild

54

What part of the poster tells the cost of visiting the Wildlife Adventure Park?

(A) The pictures of animals

(B) The park hours

(C) The price of general admission

(D) The address of the park